The Puzzles of
St. Patrick:
From Slave to Saint

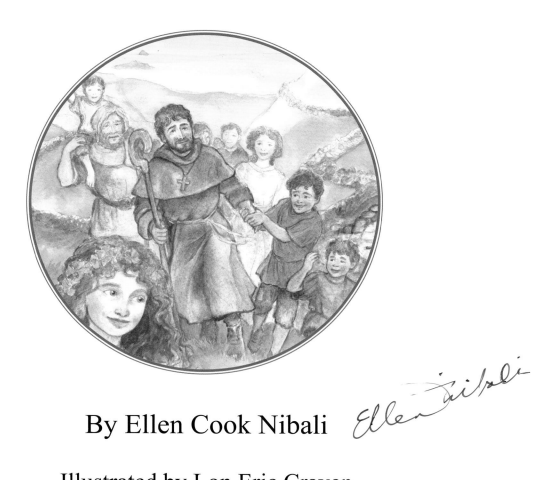

By Ellen Cook Nibali

Illustrated by Lon Eric Craven

Fairland Books
West Friendship, Maryland

To remarkable Ken,
and my parents Eleanor & Fraise,
who gave me Irish roots
– e.c.n.

For my gracious wife Melody
and our 'Irish' children
– l.e.c.

NOTES

The first surprise about St. Patrick is that he was born a 4th century Briton and Roman citizen in the waning days of the Roman empire. Kidnapped and carried off to Ireland as a child, he was enslaved for six years. After a daring escape, he made the astounding decision to return and convert the Irish, ultimately becoming their bishop. At the time, striking off to the wilderness to convert barbarians was simply not done. In the end, this trail-blazing Christian was declared a saint by popular acclaim and today is the patron saint of Ireland.

Patrick's adventures survive to this day in copies of his two letters. The complex letter known as the *Confession* defends his life's work from detractors, while sprinkled with incomplete but tantalizing accounts. In his fiery *Epistle*, he blasts the Britain warlord Coroticus, a nominal Christian, for enslaving and killing newly baptized Irish. Not intended to be autobiography, the letters leave many mystifying questions unanswered.

To emphasize the real man, the author relied on Patrick's letters almost exclusively. One undocumented yet traditional tale is included at the end to connect a wee bit to the popularized St. Patrick of today.

The Puzzles of St. Patrick: from Slave to Saint

by Ellen Cook Nibali
Illustrated by Lon Eric Craven

Library of Congress Control Number: 2013944937

(Summary: Patrick's biography, from life of privilege through slavery, escape,
and return to Ireland.)
[1. Patrick, Saint—Bio—Juvenile literature. 2. Christian saints. 3. Slavery—Biography. 4. Ireland.
5. Saint Patrick's Day.]
ISBN- 978-0-9818154-2-8

Copyright 2014 by Ellen Cook Nibali
Printed and bound in the United States of America

To order additional copies, please go to: www.fairlandbooks.com

Fairland Books
P.O. Box 63
West Friendship, Maryland 21794

On the isle of Britain in olden days, a lad had a life so easy he never gave it a thought.

Patrick's noble parents loved him. Servants waited upon him.

Patrick only half-listened to his teachers and closed his ears to his church elders. Why, he never gave himself a thought.

In those days, raiders sailed the sea between Britain and the next island, a wild and dangerous place called Ireland. The raiders stole whatever they could get their hands on — food, animals, even people. Patrick didn't give that a thought either.

Until, one night, they stole Patrick.

Patrick was bound tight, tossed into a boat, and carried over the sea to Ireland, whose people did not know God.

There he was sold to a master. From that day on, Patrick had to work from sun up to sun down, and not a thing could he do about it.

Patrick was a slave.

His master put him to work as a
shepherd. Suddenly Patrick had a whole
flock of sheep to think about. Patrick
grew to be brave and smart and kind.

But the life of a slave meant cold and hunger and loneliness. How he longed to return home.

One day, Patrick remembered something he had been taught: He was not alone. God was with him. God the Father, Son, and Holy Spirit was always there.

After that, Patrick talked to God every day. More and more the love of God came to him. Sometimes he prayed one hundred times a day and almost as many times at night.

One night, God spoke back. "Soon you will return home. Look, your ship is ready."

The ship was two hundred miles away. Patrick did not know how to get there. He did not know anyone who would help him. How could he do it?

This was a puzzle.

Patrick did not have the answer, but he trusted God and ran away from his master.

Patrick ran and hid, hid and ran, so his angry master could not capture and punish him. Never was he afraid.

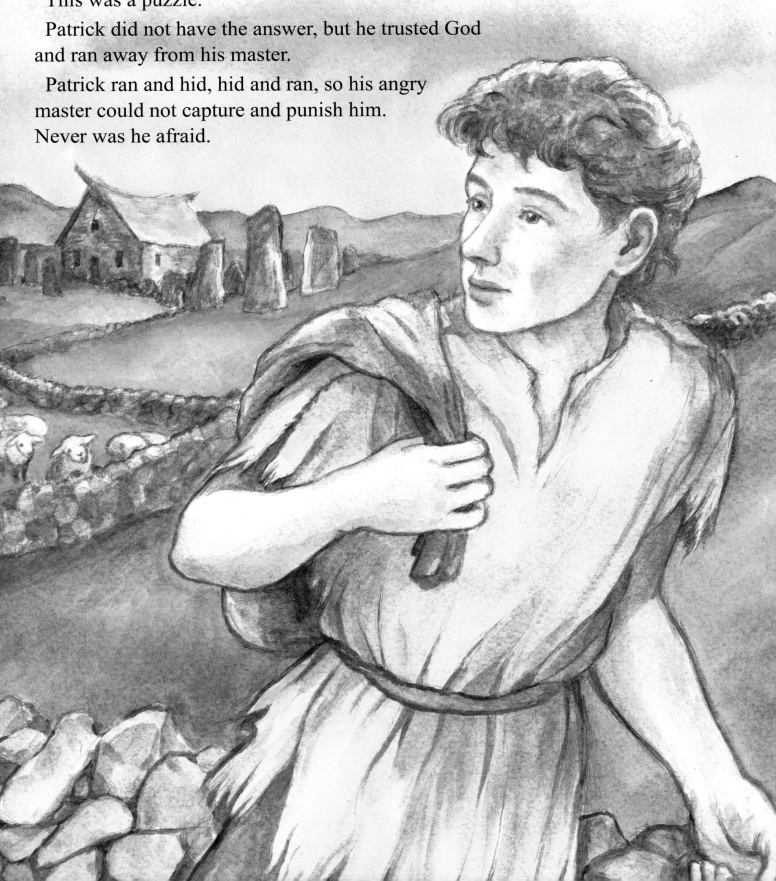

Patrick found the ship just as God said. It was about to set sail for Patrick's homeland, but the ship's captain refused to take Patrick aboard. "You cannot go with us!" he said.

Patrick turned back, puzzling as he went, "God, I did as you told me. Now what?"

Before he even finished his prayer, he heard a noise behind him. Was someone after him?

"Come quickly!" It was a sailor calling. The captain had changed his mind. Patrick was going home!

When the ship landed, the shore was strangely empty. Not a single person could they find, nor anything to eat. For twenty-eight days they wandered, until their food ran out.

"You told us your God is great and all powerful," the captain said angrily. "Why not pray for us? We are about to starve."

The hungry sailors looked to Patrick.

This puzzle was easy to solve.

"Nothing is impossible for God," Patrick said. "This day we shall have food."

Before long, a rumbling sound came closer and closer. Down the road thundered a herd of pigs. What a feast they made for the starving men!

The wanderers had so much food, it lasted until they found their way.

Home and freedom at last! Patrick's family
and friends could not believe their eyes.

"We thought we would never see you again!
No one escapes from Ireland." They all
welcomed Patrick home like a son.

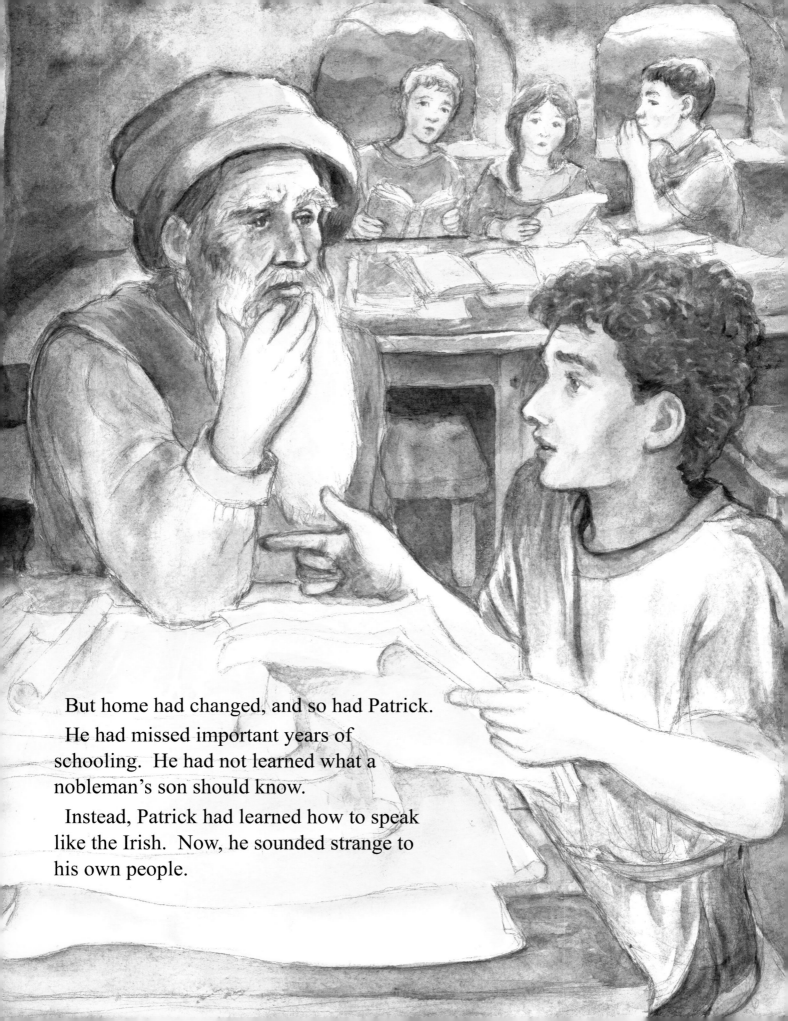

But home had changed, and so had Patrick.

He had missed important years of schooling. He had not learned what a nobleman's son should know.

Instead, Patrick had learned how to speak like the Irish. Now, he sounded strange to his own people.

One night Patrick had a dream. In it, an Irishman brought him so many letters Patrick could not count them all. He opened one and began to read, when suddenly the voices of the Irish cried out, begging Patrick to return. "Holy boy, walk among us once again."

Return to Ireland? The thought made Patrick's heart hurt. But he felt God urging him: Tell the Irish about me. Show them how much I love them.

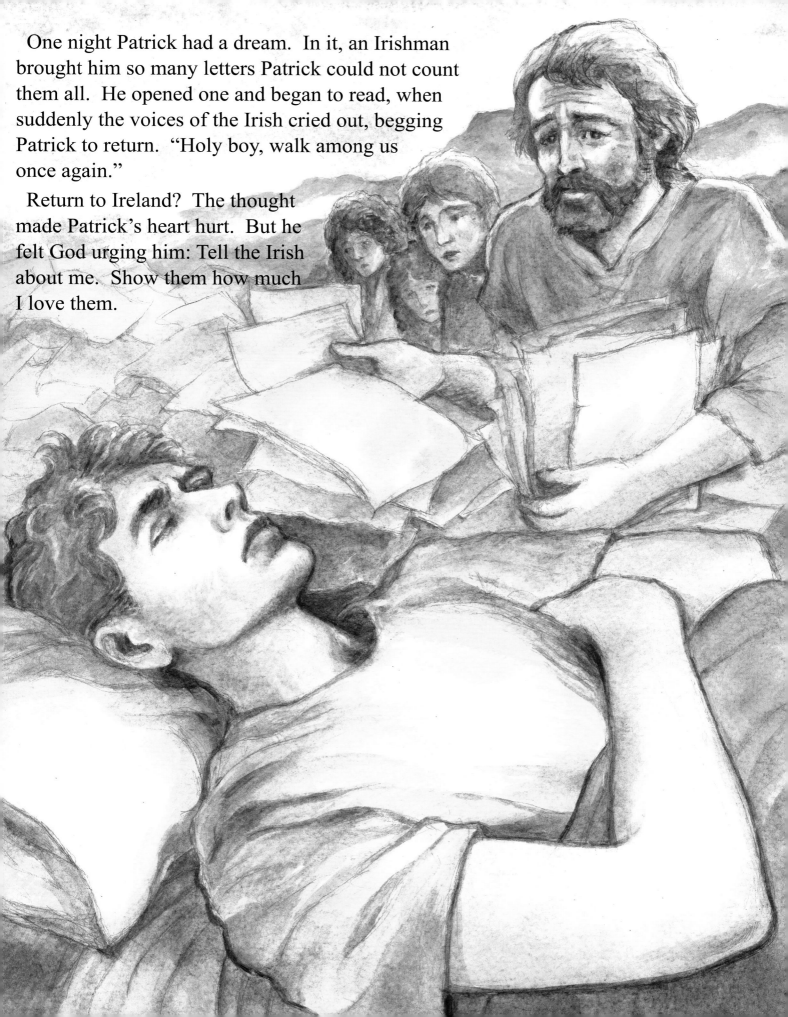

Should I go back? Patrick wondered. The Irish could make me a slave again. They might kill me for running away.

This was Patrick's hardest puzzle of all.

"I am returning to Ireland," Patrick announced.

His people were astonished. "The Irish made you a slave!" they protested. "Ireland is the end of the earth. You cannot go back!"

But Patrick had decided.

Before he went, Patrick had to learn more about God. He studied and practiced. He sold everything he owned. After many years, he was ready.

The hills of Ireland looked
green and inviting, but
Patrick knew many dangers
lay hidden there and many
puzzles lay ahead.

Off he set to face them.

Some Irish people remembered Patrick. They understood when he spoke to them. Instead of returning him to his master, they listened to what Patrick had to say about God.

But it was not easy.

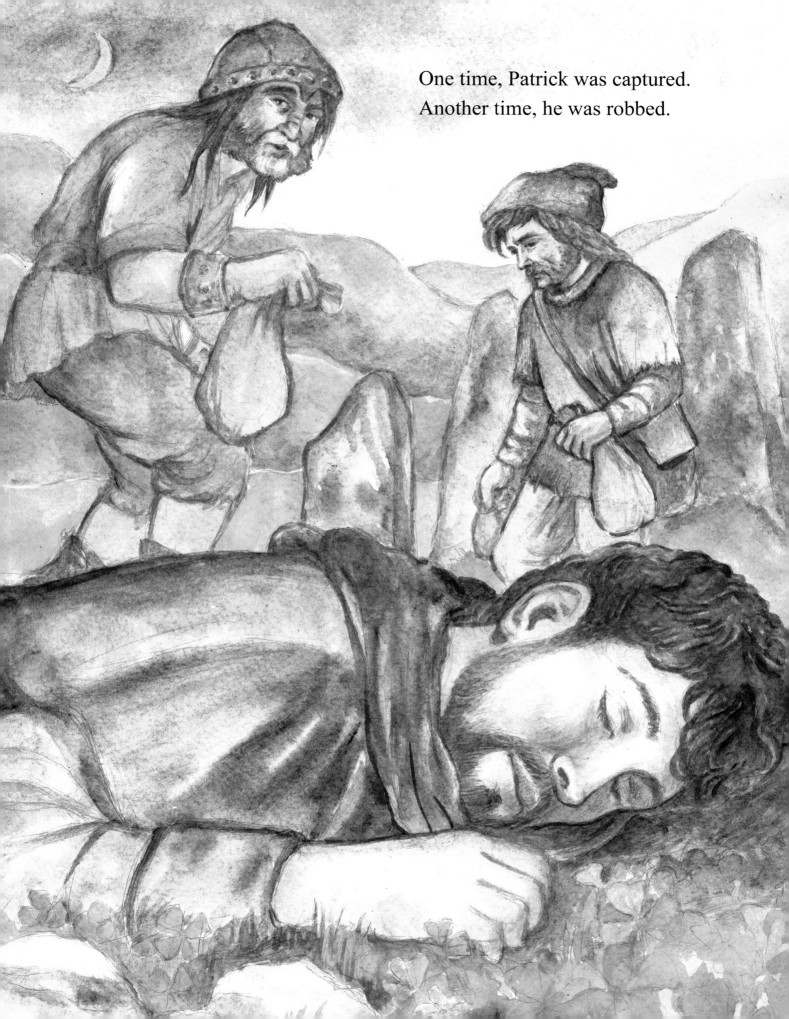

One time, Patrick was captured.
Another time, he was robbed.

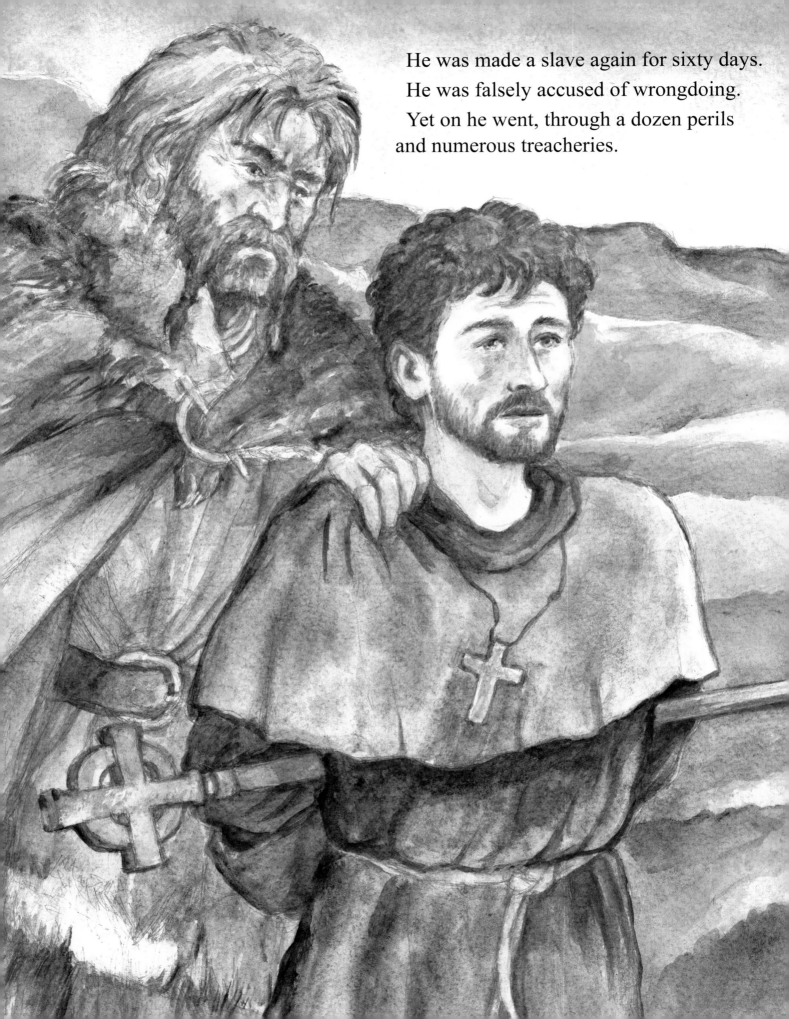

He was made a slave again for sixty days.
He was falsely accused of wrongdoing.
Yet on he went, through a dozen perils
and numerous treacheries.

For over thirty years, Patrick traveled far and wide to reach the people of Ireland. One by one, the people learned to love God. Patrick always had a special place in his heart for the slaves.

Word about Patrick spread, and others helped him. He was made a bishop, an important church leader.

Patrick never returned to his old country. Ireland became his home for the rest of his life.

When Patrick died, the people declared him Saint Patrick. To remember him always, March 17th was named St. Patrick's Day.

Everyone wanted to hear more and more about the good St. Patrick. Some stories were made up about him. Parts may be true, but no one knows for sure.

One favorite story says that when Patrick went back to Ireland, he faced a big puzzle.

Patrick told the people about his three-part God who loved them: God the Father, God the Son, and God the Holy Spirit.

"How can there be one God who is three Gods?" the people asked. They shook their heads. "One cannot be three."

People began to turn away. They were puzzled, and Patrick was puzzled, too. He could not fail the Irish people. He hung his head. How could he find a way to reach their hearts?

And there it was, growing at his feet. "See this shamrock?" he said. "This is one shamrock, but it has three leaves. God is like that, three in one."

Then the people weren't puzzled
anymore — and neither was St. Patrick.